To Robbie Griffey

CANCER

A guide to living your best astrological life

STELLA ANDROMEDA

ILLUSTRATED BY EVI O. STUDIO

Hardie Grant

BOOKS

Introduction   7

I.
Get to Know Cancer

Cancer characteristics   31
Physical Cancer   34
How Cancer communicates   37
Cancer careers   38
How Cancer chimes   41
Who loves whom?   44

II.
The Cancer Deep Dive

The Cancer home   55
Self-care   57
Food and cooking   59
How Cancer handles money   61
How Cancer handles the boss   62
What is Cancer like to live with?   65
How to handle a break-up   66
How Cancer wants to be loved   69
Cancer's sex life   72

III.

Give Me More

Your birth chart   76
The Moon effect   80
The 10 planets   83
The four elements   89
Cardinal, fixed and mutable signs   92
The 12 houses   95
The ascendant   101
Saturn return   103
Mercury retrograde   104

Further reading   108
Acknowledgements   109
About the author   111

Introduction

Inscribed on the forecourt of the ancient Greek temple of Apollo at Delphi are the words 'know thyself'. This is one of the 147 Delphic maxims, or rules to live by, attributed to Apollo himself, and was later extended by the philosopher Socrates to the sentence, 'The unexamined life is not worth living.'

People seek a variety of ways of knowing themselves, of coming to terms with life and trying to find ways to understand the challenges of human existence, often through therapy or belief systems like organised religion. These are ways in which we strive to understand the relationships we have with ourselves and others better, seeking out particular tools that enable us to do so.

As far as systems of understanding human nature and experience go, astrology has much to offer through its symbolic use of the constellations of the heavens, the depictions of the zodiac signs, the planets and their energetic effects. Many people find accessing this information and harnessing its potential a useful way of thinking about how to manage their lives more effectively.

What is astrology?

In simple terms, astrology is the study and interpretation of how the planets can influence us, and the world in which we live, through an understanding of their positions at a specific place in time. The practice of astrology relies on a combination of factual knowledge of the characteristics of these positions and their psychological interpretation.

Astrology is less of a belief system and more of a tool for living, from which ancient and established wisdom can be drawn. Any of us can learn to use astrology, not so much for divination or telling the future, but as a guidebook that provides greater insight and a more thoughtful way of approaching life. Timing is very much at the heart of astrology, and knowledge of planetary configurations and their relationship to each other at specific moments in time can assist in helping us with the timing of some of our life choices and decisions.

Knowing when major life shifts can occur – because of particular planetary configurations such as a Saturn return (see page 103) or Mercury retrograde (see page 104) – or what it means to have Venus in your seventh house (see pages 85 and 98), while recognising the specific characteristics of your sign, are all tools that you can use to your advantage. Knowledge is power, and astrology can be a very powerful supplement to approaching life's ups and downs and any relationships we form along the way.

Cancer

The 12 signs of the zodiac

Each sign of the zodiac has a range of recognisable characteristics, shared by people born under that sign. This is your Sun sign, which you probably already know – and the usual starting point from which we each begin to explore our own astrological paths. Sun sign characteristics can be strongly exhibited in an individual's make-up; however, this is only part of the picture.

Usually, how we appear to others is tempered by the influence of other factors – and these are worth bearing in mind. Your ascendant sign is equally important, as is the positioning of your Moon. You can also look to your opposite sign to see what your Sun sign may need a little more of, to balance its characteristics.

After getting to know your Sun sign in the first part of this book, you might want to dive into the Give Me More section (see pages 74–105) to start to explore all the particulars of your birth chart. These will give you far greater insight into the myriad astrological influences that may play out in your life.

Sun signs

It takes 365 (and a quarter, to be precise) days for the Earth to orbit the Sun and in so doing, the Sun appears to us to spend a month travelling through each sign of the zodiac. Your Sun sign is therefore an indication of the sign that the Sun was travelling through at the time of your birth. Knowing what Sun signs you and your family, friends and lovers are provides you with just the beginning of the insights into character and personality that astrology can help you discover.

On the cusp

For those for whom a birthday falls close to the end of one Sun sign and the beginning of another, it's worth knowing what time you were born. There's no such thing, astrologically, as being 'on the cusp' – because the signs begin at a specific time on a specific date, although this can vary a little year on year. If you are not sure, you'll need to know your birth date, birth time and birth place to work out accurately to which Sun sign you belong. Once you have these, you can consult an astrologer or run your details through an online astrology site program (see page 108) to give you the most accurate birth chart possible.

Taurus

The bull

*

21 APRIL–20 MAY

Grounded, sensual and appreciative of bodily pleasures, Taurus is a fixed earth sign endowed by its ruling planet Venus with grace and a love of beauty, despite its depiction as a bull. Generally characterised by an easy and uncomplicated, if occasionally stubborn, approach to life, Taurus' opposite sign is watery Scorpio.

Aries

The ram

*

21 MARCH–20 APRIL

Astrologically the first sign of the zodiac, Aries appears alongside the vernal (or spring) equinox. A cardinal fire sign, depicted by the ram, it is the sign of beginnings and ruled by planet Mars, which represents a dynamic ability to meet challenges energetically and creatively. Its opposite sign is airy Libra.

Gemini

The twins

★

21 MAY-20 JUNE

A mutable air sign symbolised by the twins, Gemini tends to see both sides of an argument, its speedy intellect influenced by its ruling planet Mercury. Tending to fight shy of commitment, this sign also epitomises a certain youthfulness of attitude. Its opposite sign is fiery Sagittarius.

Cancer

The crab

★

21 JUNE-21 JULY

Depicted by the crab and the tenacity of its claws, Cancer is a cardinal water sign, emotional and intuitive, its sensitivity protected by its shell. Ruled by the maternal Moon, the shell also represents the security of home, to which Cancer is committed. Its opposite sign is earthy Capricorn.

Leo

The lion

22 JULY–21 AUGUST

A fixed fire sign, ruled by the Sun, Leo loves to shine and is an idealist at heart, positive and generous to a fault. Depicted by the lion, Leo can roar with pride and be confident and uncompromising, with a great faith and trust in humanity. Its opposite sign is airy Aquarius.

Virgo

The virgin

22 AUGUST–21 SEPTEMBER

Traditionally represented as a maiden or virgin, this mutable earth sign is observant, detail oriented and tends towards self-sufficiency. Ruled by Mercury, Virgos benefit from a sharp intellect that can be self-critical, while often being very health conscious. Its opposite sign is watery Pisces.

Scorpio

The scorpion

22 OCTOBER–21 NOVEMBER

Given to intense feelings, as
befits a fixed water sign, Scorpio
is depicted by the scorpion – linking
it to the rebirth that follows death –
and is ruled by both Pluto and Mars.
With a strong spirituality and deep
emotions, Scorpio needs security to
transform its strength. Its opposite
sign is earthy Taurus.

Libra

The scales

22 SEPTEMBER–21 OCTOBER

A cardinal air sign, ruled by Venus,
Libra is all about beauty, balance
(as depicted by the scales) and
harmony in its rather romanticised,
ideal world. With a strong aesthetic
sense, Libra can be both arty and
crafty, but also likes fairness and
can be very diplomatic. Its
opposite sign is fiery Aries.

Sagittarius

The archer

★

22 NOVEMBER–21 DECEMBER

Depicted by the archer, Sagittarius is a mutable fire sign that's all about travel and adventure, in body or mind, and is very direct in approach. Ruled by the benevolent Jupiter, Sagittarius is optimistic with lots of ideas; liking a free rein, but with a tendency to generalise. Its opposite sign is airy Gemini.

Capricorn

The goat

★

22 DECEMBER–20 JANUARY

Ruled by Saturn, Capricorn is a cardinal earth sign associated with hard work and depicted by the sure-footed and sometimes playful goat. Trustworthy and unafraid of commitment, Capricorn is often very self-sufficient and has the discipline for the freelance working life. Its opposite sign is the watery Cancer.

Aquarius

The water carrier

★

21 JANUARY–19 FEBRUARY

Confusingly, given its depiction by the water carrier, Aquarius is a fixed air sign ruled by the unpredictable Uranus, sweeping away old ideas with innovative thinking. Tolerant, open-minded and all about humanity, its vision is social with a conscience. Its opposite sign is fiery Leo.

Pisces

The fish

★

20 FEBRUARY–20 MARCH

Acutely responsive to its surroundings, Pisces is a mutable water sign depicted by two fish, swimming in opposite directions, sometimes confusing fantasy with reality. Ruled by Neptune, its world is fluid, imaginative and empathetic, often picking up on the moods of others. Its opposite sign is earthy Virgo.

Get to
I.

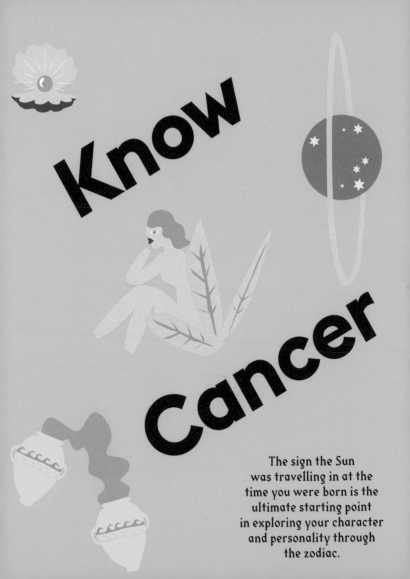

Know

Cancer

The sign the Sun
was travelling in at the
time you were born is the
ultimate starting point
in exploring your character
and personality through
the zodiac.

Cardinal water sign
depicted by the crab.

Ruled by the Moon
and its rhythms, which
also influences the tides
of the sea.

OPPOSITE SIGN

Capricorn

STATEMENT OF SELF

'I feel.'

Lucky colour

Silver is Cancer's lucky colour, including the silvery blue-green iridescence of the sea. Much like Cancer's ruler, the Moon, polished silver reflects light; and while often worn as jewellery, silver clothes and accessories will also connect to Cancer energy when you need a psychological boost and additional courage.

Lucky day

Monday. Considered to be the first day of the working week in many countries, it takes its name from *Moonday* and, in the French, *Lundi*, from *lune*, meaning Moon.

III.

Lucky gem

The pearl, with its beautiful luminescence, was thought
by the ancient Greeks to be tears of joy of the goddess of
love, Aphrodite. A symbol of purity, pearls are also thought
to reverse misfortune. The moonstone is also considered
a lucky gem for Cancerians, enhancing Moon energy and
intuition, and heralding new cycles and beginnings.

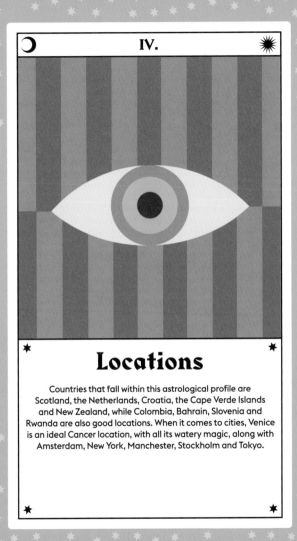

IV.

Locations

Countries that fall within this astrological profile are Scotland, the Netherlands, Croatia, the Cape Verde Islands and New Zealand, while Colombia, Bahrain, Slovenia and Rwanda are also good locations. When it comes to cities, Venice is an ideal Cancer location, with all its watery magic, along with Amsterdam, New York, Manchester, Stockholm and Tokyo.

Holidays

For many Cancerians the staycation is enticing, as they truly enjoy time spent in their home, often finding it more relaxing than struggling through an airport. But for those that do manage to actually leave the country, renting a lovely seaside villa with room for all the family on a Greek island might suit. Other destinations might find them exploring the Galapagos Islands, or turtle watching at Ras Al Jinz in Oman.

Flowers

White, sweet-scented jasmine, with its tenacity and capacity to embrace the walls of a home, and morning glory, are both Cancer flowers. Acanthus, too, with its pale white and mauve flowers, symbolises rebirth, immortality and healing.

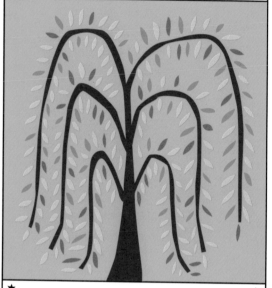

Trees

The willow tree, with its silvery green leaves trailing down towards water, is a Cancer tree, along with the silver birch with its papery bark and shimmering leaves. Other trees that have a high sap (fluid) content, like acers or elms, are also associated with this astrological sign.

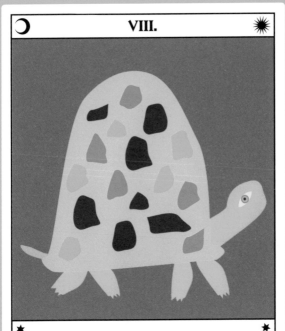

Pets

A pet turtle can be a good choice because Cancer will easily identify with this attractive creature carrying its home on its back. And because a turtle and its aquarium home require quite a lot of care, this will resonate with Cancer's need to nurture.

Parties

A beach party is right up the crab's street, dancing at the surf's edge in the moonlight. But, for Cancer, the preference is always for a gathering of close friends rather than a hoard of unknowns. In the absence of a seaside, a house party will suffice, preferably at their own home. There's bound to be lots of delicious food and perhaps a moonshine cocktail of tequila, triple sec and coconut cream, shaken with masses of ice and some lime juice.

Cancer characteristics

Loyal, kind, sympathetic – all this is true about Cancer, but they can also appear to be a little 'crabby': like the crab that depicts this sign, there is a very gentle and soft interior that occasionally needs quite a hard exterior to hide and safeguard their feelings. The crab is also at home on land and in water, so is comfortable both in the real world but also in the shifting seas of their imagination. Make no mistake, Cancer is all about feelings and, ruled by the Moon, those shifting tides of feeling can fluctuate very strongly below the surface.

Cancer is also a cardinal sign, with a strong, ambitious engagement with the real world and its inhabitants, and is very much a people person too. They are all about relationships, with their lover especially, but also their family and friends. Once they make a commitment they hang on tight, giving them that other well-known characteristic of the sign of the crab – tenacity.

Like its ruler, the Moon, Cancer can similarly appear to fluctuate in intensity – sometimes easily 'seen' and sometimes less so – which gives this sign something of a reputation for moodiness. It's not so much moodiness, but the need for occasional time out necessary to process all those feelings – retreating into their shell to do so – that can make them disappear emotionally. This detachment can disguise something of a brooder, who finds it hard to let go of worrisome thoughts. There can be an element of secrecy, too, as they are quite capable of hiding feelings and information and won't give much away unless it's safe to do so.

Regardless of their sex, Cancer tends to have a strongly nurturing, maternal side, because the Moon is gendered female in its attributes. They are often depicted as the carers of the zodiac, and this can be seen in Cancer's love of family and the ability to create a wonderful home life, but also in the way this care is extended to other people (or animals). They often relate easily to children, and can be nostalgic about their own childhood, which can also create a potentially child-like need for security but, because they are also a cardinal sign, they can be very pragmatic and are as capable of creating this for themselves as for others. No walkover; there's a real strength and resilience to Cancer that's not always so obvious from their softer, more evidently intuitive side.

TEMPERING THE WATER

The key characteristics of any Sun sign can be balanced out (or sometimes reinforced) by the characteristics of other signs in the same birth chart, particularly those of the ascendant and the Moon. So if someone doesn't appear to be typical of their Sun sign, that's why. However, those nascent Cancer aspects will always be there as a key influence, informing an individual's approach to life.

Physical
Cancer

Cancer can sometimes look rather tentative, an observer standing to the side of the action, or coming at it from an angle, but definitely taking it all in. This doesn't arise from lack of confidence necessarily, but from an interested, observing, considered viewpoint. But once they've got their bearings they're happy to front up, even if they come at it sideways, like the crab itself. In spite of this tendency towards prevarication, Cancer often has a direct, sometimes piercing gaze as they just can't help weighing up the situation, scanning the vibes like a psychic. Until they're sure of what they want to say, however, they often hold their own counsel.

Health

The belly is ruled by the astrological sign of the crab, and all that ruminating and worrying they do can sometimes play havoc with their digestive system, making them prone to ulcers and other stomach problems. A delicate stomach can also be aggravated by over-indulgence of both food and alcohol, and Cancer will often comfort eat when they're anxious, which means that there can be a tendency to carry a little too much weight. For women, the breasts, too, which link to the maternal nurturing epitomised by Cancer, may also have problems with cysts and other issues, so good self-care and regular checks are important (as they are for every woman).

Exercise

This is the sign that has the tenacity for something like a marathon, or even a triathlon that combines exercise on land and water where a crab is equally at home, but their innate domesticity may find them on an exercise bike in their bedroom instead. Cancer likes to connect their mind to their bodies, too, even if only to keep focused, so some sort of regular exercise should find its way into their schedule and could include some Hatha yoga and breath work to balance out more energetic, aerobic activity.

How Cancer communicates

Cancer is a great and, more importantly, a genuine listener and responds on the basis of what they've actually heard. They bring all their attention to a situation and focus on the other person, because this is also one of the ways they demonstrate that they care. Intuitive to a fault, Cancer can also appear to read other people like a book and often responds to unspoken vibes with uncanny accuracy, which can sometimes be a bit disconcerting for their lover or friend. They know the value of listening attentively, and are often sought out for their advice, which is usually very thoughtful and appropriate. Sometimes, however, Cancer can forget that not everyone else is as intuitive as they are, and can feel resentful if they feel they're not being heard. Then they can retreat into their shell, appearing cut off and moody, but really just needing some time and genuine attention to coax them out again.

Cancer
careers

Given their enjoyment of the domestic, Cancer is very happy doing home-based work, such as freelance writing or running an online business, especially as they are one of the signs with enough self-discipline to be their own boss. Writing in particular can be an extension of a fluid imagination, which Cancer has in abundance. Writing also requires the tenacity to sit alone for long stretches of time, buried in an idea much like a crab buries itself in the sand.

The caring and service professions are also very attractive to Cancer, as these play to a genuine interest in taking care of others. This could mean the hospitality industry, working in restaurants, hotels or holiday resorts. Cancer's innate empathy and ability to listen and think through someone else's problems makes being a psychologist, therapist or relationship counsellor an option, while medicine and nursing combine this ability with more pragmatic hands-on skills. Their ability to relate well to children and young people also makes teaching or childcare a possibility.

How
Cancer
chimes

A popular friend, because that gift for listening is highly prized even in a busy world, Cancer is often a best friend before they become a lover. They attach themselves securely to people they're attracted to and will wait until the moment is right to make their, often sideways, move. Cancer is no pushover, even though they are a cautious, sensitive water sign, because they are also a cardinal sign with a strong sense of what they are entitled to, so are happy to take the initiative when the time is right. Once Cancer turns their attention to someone, their decision to move from friend to lover is rooted in a conviction that can overcome all obstacles.

The Cancer woman

The epitome of feminine, the Cancer woman may seem quietly flirtatious but she's also deeply sensual and, once she falls in love, her commitment is strong. Loyalty is a key component as long as her trust isn't betrayed, and she doesn't take kindly to being fooled. That quiet demeanour can be deceptive, because beneath that softness lies a steely resolve to make a difference and get things done.

NOTABLE CANCER WOMEN

Princess Diana was hugely empathetic on a world stage, but also had that fabulously intimate and feminine way of looking up flirtatiously from under her eyelashes. Actor Margot Robbie with her own production company, singer Ariana Grande and activist and campaigner Malala Yousafzai, all embody a remarkable strength of character that gets things done, on their own terms and in their own way.

The Cancer man

The Cancer man takes his role as protector pretty seriously and will sometimes appear rather old-fashioned in their approach to do so. Romantic gestures are genuine but may also serve to test the water, because if he is to risk his affections he needs to be sure, as Cancer takes any rejection hard. This mix of masculine sensitivity is very attractive but can sometimes be tricky to balance.

NOTABLE CANCER MEN

Writer Ernest Hemingway's bravura masked a sensitive soul, and we saw the same trait in actor Robin Williams, who also felt things very deeply. Tom Cruise and Prince William are typical Cancer males, combining a love of action with a need for romantic gesture and a harmonious domestic life.

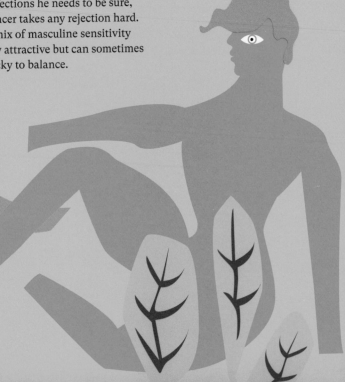

Who love

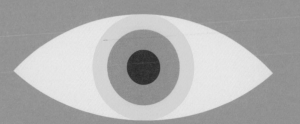

whom?

Cancer &
Aries

The sexual attraction
between this fire and water sign
combination can be steamy,
but Aries may find Cancer's
tendency towards defensiveness
inhibiting, while the crab's liking
for domesticity can fuel
Aries' desire for escape.

Cancer &
Taurus

Both find the affection they
seek in each other and are
sexually well suited. Cancer can
bring out a more imaginative
side to steady Taurus and, in
return, Cancer's tendency
towards moodiness is well
grounded and tolerated.

Cancer &
Gemini

Although initially attracted
to Gemini, they can be just too
fickle for the security-seeking
crab, and their intellect tends
to clash with Cancer's intuitive
take on life although that
intriguing airiness can ventilate
some of their thinking.

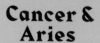

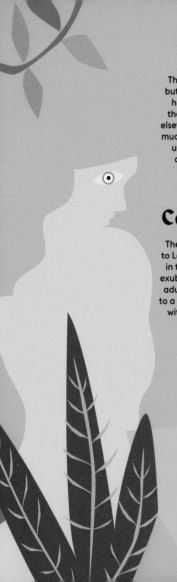

Cancer & Cancer

They understand each other
but, with so much in common,
how will it pan out? In bed,
they're a sensual match, but
elsewhere there may just be too
much possessiveness and need,
unless they're able to take
a step back occasionally.

Cancer & Leo

There's a wonderful optimism
to Leo that attracts Cancer, but
in the long run that continual
exuberance and need for public
adulation can be troublesome
to a soul prone to sensitivity and
with a need for reassurance.

Cancer & Virgo

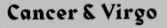

Because Virgo's attention to detail
chimes with Cancer's need for security,
and the balance between emotion
and intellect are there, this is
a harmonious and affectionate
bond from the start.

Cancer &
Scorpio

These two signs understand each other, and Cancer's commitment and affection make Scorpio feel very secure, reducing the potential sting in their tail and allowing for the physical and emotional intimacy they both thrive on.

Cancer &
Libra

When Cancer's emotional take on love meets Libra's intellectual need for balance this can cause friction, and understanding each other's needs can be tricky. A commitment to creating a beautiful home helps, but it may not be enough.

Cancer &
Sagittarius

Cancer tends to find this fire sign's flighty nature makes them feel too insecure, while their more sensitive, domestic side tends to grate on freedom-loving Sagittarius' nerves. In the long term, they make better friends than lovers.

Cancer &
Aquarius

Way too prone to be detached,
intellectual and unpredictable to meet
Cancer's basic need for attention,
Aquarius may be of interest sexually
but isn't often emotionally engaged
enough to allow this to endure
much past the bedroom.

Cancer & Pisces

Both imaginative water signs
but in different ways – one a doer
and the other a worker – they are
also sensually compatible, Cancer's
protectiveness happily supporting
Pisces' romantic vision. They
understand and work well together.

Cancer &
Capricorn

Astrological opposites always
tend to attract, at least initially,
but Capricorn's reserve and
self-reliance can be interpreted
as rejection by Cancer, which
makes for an uneasy
alliance over time.

Cancer love-o-meter

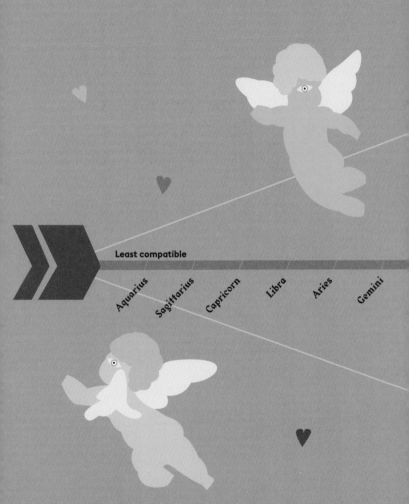

Least compatible

Aquarius   Sagittarius   Capricorn   Libra   Aries   Gemini

Most compatible

Cancer Leo Taurus Pisces Virgo Scorpio

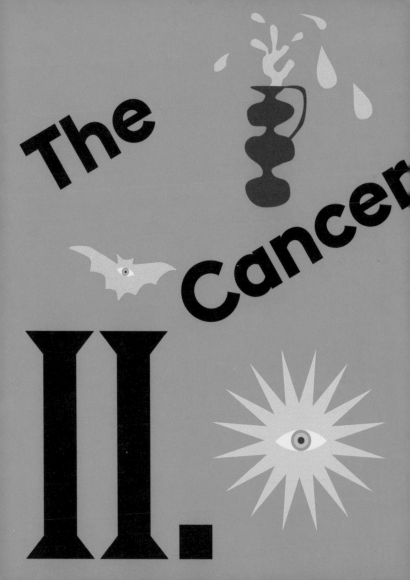

The Cancer

II.

Deep Dive

In this section, dive deeper into the ways in which your Sun sign might be driving you or holding you back, and start to think about how you might use this knowledge to inform your path.

The Cancer home

Home for Cancer is where the heart is, so it's likely to be a refuge, reflected in the serenity of its colours and lack of clutter. But there is nothing hyper-stylised about Cancer's home. It's all about comfort and gentle accommodation, with no harsh lighting or discordant aspects. There's often lots of photos of family and friends, going back through time. Here's where Cancer can feel safe and shut out the rest of the world.

Sanded oak floors, large seascapes in driftwood frames, globe lighting or moon-shaped light shades and muslin drapes, there may be a maritime or beach cabin feel to the decor, but often with a warm, glowing hearth. That fire is likely to be an important focus, too, because, in spite of Cancer being a water sign, their cardinal aspect means that they believe in what is fundamental to family life, represented by the hearth and heart of the home. Even if it's the home of a Cancer man, there are likely to be feminine touches like soft towels in the bathroom, fresh flowers or cushions on the sofa.

TOP TIPS FOR
CANCER SELF-CARE

★ Alternate water-based exercise,
like swimming, with a more
grounded yoga practice to
help balance a broody mind.

★ Peppermint tea can be
a good aid to digestion.

★ Take a walk along the sea
shore to reconnect to the
natural environment.

Self-care

Other-care is so much easier than self-care to Cancer, who tends to neglect their own needs while ensuring others are looked after. Prevention being better than cure, Cancer should be encouraged to take regular exercise that takes them out of their minds for a while and relaxes their bodies. Often as happy in water as on land, half an hour spent swimming pool lengths will help exercise the body while calming the mind – the perfect antidote to all that thinking.

It's important for Cancer to schedule proper time out to balance their close emotional involvement with others, to gain perspective and also to recover, especially if they work in a demanding, full-on job, like teaching or nursing. Otherwise stress, exhaustion and burnout can be a problem. Practising mindfulness meditation, perhaps in conjunction with some Hatha yoga, to harness their breath and instil calming thoughts when needed, will also help. This should also help relieve those stomach knots that can cause digestive problems. And to feel soothed and cherished, after having soothed and cherished everyone else? An hour's run followed by a full-body massage with therapeutic jasmine and sandalwood oils, to the sound of sea waves, should do the trick.

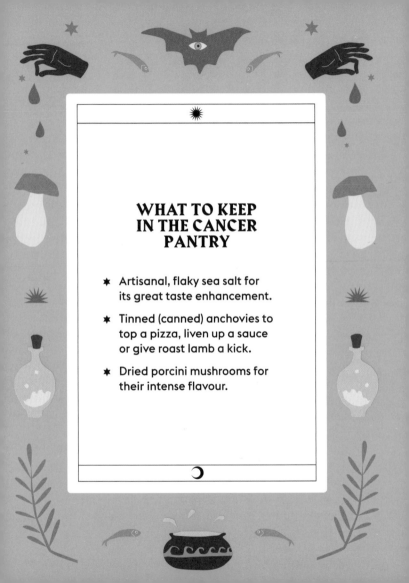

WHAT TO KEEP IN THE CANCER PANTRY

★ Artisanal, flaky sea salt for its great taste enhancement.

★ Tinned (canned) anchovies to top a pizza, liven up a sauce or give roast lamb a kick.

★ Dried porcini mushrooms for their intense flavour.

Food
and
cooking

What better way to show love for Cancer than to cook? Not for them the frozen meal or home delivery – that Italian mama dispensing spaghetti Bolognese to all and sundry is the epitome of the sign of the crab and a well-stocked fridge and provision cupboard is highly likely in Cancer's home. Their attitude to what they eat is robust and appreciative, even if they are sometimes prone to food sensitivities. Even so, Cancer is unlikely to be faddy about food or follow prescriptive diets like veganism, as they don't embody a particularly puritanical streak and their sensual side relishes the pleasure of preparing, cooking and eating too much for that.

This is the man who's happy to patiently prepare risotto from scratch, handmake exquisite vegetable samosas or even gluten-free bread sauce, to demonstrate his love, or the woman whose choux pastry for her signature chocolate eclairs is both delicious and legendary.

TOP TIPS FOR
CANCER'S MONEY

* Trust your instincts:
  sometimes you have to
  speculate to accumulate.

* Real estate investment is a
  secure option for Cancerian
  nest eggs.

* Don't forget to also have funds
  saved to use to have fun.

How Cancer handles money

Along with protecting their family, Cancer likes to protect their future, so when it comes to money, saving some for a rainy day comes pretty naturally. Money represents security in all sorts of ways, and Cancer can be very shrewd in its acquisition, often through good business deals and working hard. This sign is generous but not profligate, and can usually be relied upon to ensure outgoings are a reflection of income, seldom spending beyond their means and generally paying off their credit card as they go.

Cancer also tends to hang on to money, not because they're mean but because they need to feel protected and however much they have in the bank, they will often worry that it's never enough. Spending for fun is generally in a way that encompasses family or friends, often through socialising at home or facilitating group gatherings which holds more attraction than the accumulation of bling.

How Cancer handles the boss

There is always the temptation for Cancer to try to mother everyone. Sure, if you're a PA to someone who expects their coffee made a certain way and their dry cleaning picked up, then that's just a part of the job. But if you are a team player, then making the tea for others should only be done when you're making one for yourself. Otherwise, you could find your role diminished or your time misused by workmates. Bottom line, your job is to deliver on the job you've been employed to do, and priority must be given to that, rather than to the emotional life of other staff.

A preoccupation with the emotional lives of your colleagues can also lead to time-wasting gossip, which can sometimes backfire. And if your boss has shared secrets, or you know about their extra-marital affair, they may come to resent Cancer's intuitive ways, which is never a helpful work scenario. So always keep in mind that Cancer needs to balance their empathetic traits with a hard-nosed focus on getting the job done. Sometimes it's hard for Cancer to leave a job, in order to advance their career or prospects, but being straight with the boss about this will help.

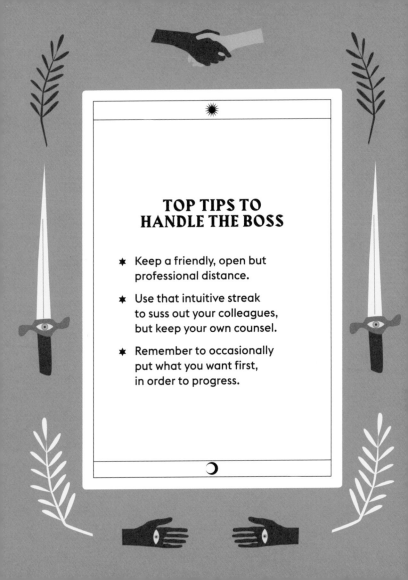

TOP TIPS TO
HANDLE THE BOSS

★ Keep a friendly, open but professional distance.

★ Use that intuitive streak to suss out your colleagues, but keep your own counsel.

★ Remember to occasionally put what you want first, in order to progress.

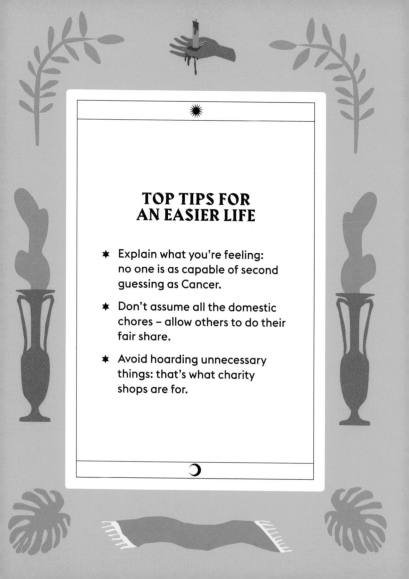

TOP TIPS FOR
AN EASIER LIFE

★ Explain what you're feeling:
  no one is as capable of second
  guessing as Cancer.

★ Don't assume all the domestic
  chores – allow others to do their
  fair share.

★ Avoid hoarding unnecessary
  things: that's what charity
  shops are for.

What is Cancer like to live with?

Although domestically orientated, Cancer isn't necessarily the easiest sign to live with because their inner life is so active, it's not always obvious to housemates or partners what's going on inside that imaginative, intuitive mind. A quiet mood could mean happy introspection, thinking through a piece of work, or feeling upset. And while they find security in family and friends, Cancerians also need quite a lot of downtime to process their feelings, sometimes to the exasperation of those around them who can easily misinterpret what's going on.

Cancer is also the proverbial collector, and this may show itself in a sentimental attachment to possessions that have no obvious meaning to anyone else but are important to them. So that collection of theatre programmes is essential, as is that chipped mug from childhood. Conversely, when the mood strikes, they can be abruptly, ruthlessly, minimalist and have a massive clear out. Interestingly, Cancer also has a tendency to collect people, and they often have lots of friends of different ages and from different backgrounds.

How to handle a break-up

It can be very, very hard for Cancer to let go at the end of a relationship or love affair, irrespective of whether they are the one doing the breaking up. The problem with this rather indecisive style is that it can send out mixed messages and cause more hurt to both parties in the long run. And in a reaction to all this emotion, the crab can retreat and scuttle off, completely disappearing emotionally in order to try and cope.

They may also do this if they are the one who is dumped, refusing any love and support from well-meaning family or friends, shutting them out while they hurt inside. It's very much all or nothing with Cancer, it's the way they cope, but emotions need to be expressed and they will, in the end, do so and move on.

TOP TIPS FOR
AN EASIER BREAK-UP

★ Be clear about accepting when
  a relationship is over and then
  let it go.

★ Don't shut out friends; find
  a trusted shoulder to lean on.

★ Implement that self-care
  strategy to get through the
  first few days and weeks.

How Cancer wants to be loved

Often underestimated is the cautious side of Cancer, edging towards the water and then retreating is a typical characteristic when it comes to approaching love, so they have to be offered lots of reassurance – proof that it's worth the risk of getting wet. They never act before they're sure but when they are, that's it: committed. However tentative they are, though, once committed, Cancer will hold on tight and is loyal to a fault. Of course, then their expectation is to receive the same and they won't take kindly to being messed around. Never treat a Cancer mean to keep them keen; they don't like it and will be off. Game playing isn't particularly their style.

So, what is Cancer looking for? Sureness and kindness are key words; they need to know their partner cares. This highly sensual sign needs real passion, too, and you can't fake it, or Cancer will suss that out and any insincerity to boot. It's just that for any sort of transcendence in the bedroom there has to be a sense of security in the rest of the home, which is key for this creature ruled by the Moon and all its fluctuating influence. And romance is important, too, especially on first dates, where the moonlit mood weaves its own magic. Inevitably, one way to Cancer's heart is through their stomach, and the offer of a home-cooked meal can be even more welcome than one in a restaurant.

TOP TIPS FOR
LOVING CANCER

* Compliments are great,
  but they must be sincere.

* Flirting is fine, as long as
  it's only with them.

* Don't mistake reticence
  for lack of interest – Cancer
  takes a while before declaring
  their intention.

Cancer's sex life

In the bedroom, Cancer is a sensitive lover, happily focused on their partner's pleasure, empathetic and sometimes appearing almost too anxious to please, forgetting that sex is a two-way affair and that receiving creates as much pleasure as giving. This confident exterior is partly a defence, shielding a more sensitive, gentle soul. The more secure Cancer is, the more likely they are to relax and lose themselves in the moment; swept away from their immediate physical self on a tide of emotion.

Getting close to Cancer takes time, but it's always worth it. They like to take their time in the bedroom and it's seldom a quick event, more often a sensuous affair, and they are capable of being highly imaginative and playful once they're sure of their partner's commitment. Of course, casual sex can happen but primarily Cancer is all about the relationship in which sex can exist and flourish and communicate real feeling. Massage can be a key element of foreplay for Cancer, as attention to the physical body helps them open up and get past that protective, outer shell.

Me

More

Your Sun sign never shows you the whole picture. In this section, learn how to read the nuances of your birth chart and discover a whole new level of astrological insight.

Your
birth
chart

Your birth chart is a snapshot of a particular moment, in a particular place, at the precise moment of your birth and is therefore completely individual to you. It's like a blueprint, a map, a statement of occurrence, spelling out possible traits and influences – but it isn't your destiny. It is just a symbolic tool to which you can refer, based on the position of the planets at the time of your birth. If you can't get to an astrologer, these days anyone can get their birth chart prepared in minutes online (see page 108 for a list of websites and apps that will do it for you). Even if you don't know your exact time of birth, just knowing the date and place of birth can create the beginnings of a useful template.

Remember, nothing is intrinsically good or bad in astrology and there is no explicit timing or forecasting: it's more a question of influences and how these might play out positively or negatively. And if we have some insight, and some tools with which to approach, see or interpret our circumstances and surroundings, this gives us something to work with.

When you are reading your birth chart, it's useful to first understand all the tools of astrology available to you; not only the astrological signs and what they represent, but also the 10 planets referred to in astrology and their individual characteristics, along with the 12 houses and what they mean. Individually, these tools of astrology are of passing interest, but when you start to see how they might sit in juxtaposition to each other, then the bigger picture becomes more accessible and we begin to gain insights that can be useful to us.

Broadly speaking, each of the planets suggests a different type of energy, the astrological signs propose the various ways in which that energy might be expressed, while the houses represent areas of experience in which this expression might operate.

Next to bring into the picture are the positions of the signs at four key points: the ascendant, or rising sign, and its opposite, the descendant; and the midheaven and its opposite, the IC, not to mention the different aspects created by congregations of signs and planets.

It is now possible to see how subtle the reading of a birth chart might be and how it is infinite in its variety, and highly specific to an individual. With this information, and a working understanding of the symbolic meaning and influences of the signs, planets and houses of your unique astrological profile, you can begin to use these tools to help with decision-making and other aspects of life.

Reading your chart

If you have your birth chart prepared, either by hand or via an online program, you will see a circle divided into 12 segments, with information clustered at various points indicating the position of each zodiac sign, in which segment it appears and at what degree. Irrespective of the features that are relevant to the individual, each chart follows the same pattern when it comes to interpretation.

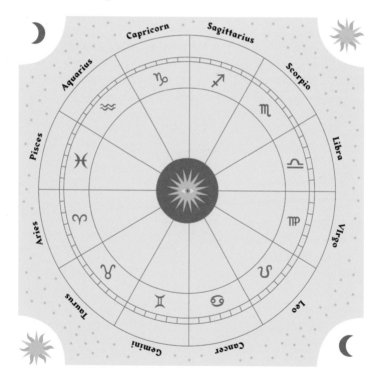

Cancer

Given the time of birth, the place of birth and the position of the planets at that moment, the birth chart, sometimes called a natal horoscope, is drawn up.

If you consider the chart as a clock face, the first house (see pages 95–99 for the astrological houses) begins at the 9, and it is from this point that, travelling anti-clockwise the chart is read from the first house, through the 12 segments of the chart to the twelfth.

The beginning point, the 9, is also the point at which the Sun rises on your life, giving you your ascendant, or rising sign, and opposite to this, at the 3 of the clock face, is your descendant sign. The midheaven point of your chart, the MC, is at 12, and its opposite, the IC, at 6 (see pages 101–102).

Understanding the significance of the characteristics of the astrological signs and the planets, their particular energies, their placements and their aspects to each other can be helpful in understanding ourselves and our relationships with others. In day-to-day life, too, the changing configuration of planets and their effects are much more easily understood with a basic knowledge of astrology, as are the recurring patterns that can sometimes strengthen and sometimes delay opportunities and possibilities. Working with, rather than against, these trends can make life more manageable and, in the last resort, more successful.

The Moon effect

If your Sun sign represents your consciousness, your life force and your individual will, then the Moon represents that side of your personality that you tend to keep rather secret or hidden. This is the realm of instinct, intuition, creativity and the unconscious, which can take you places emotionally that are sometimes hard to understand. This is what brings great subtlety and nuance to a person, way beyond just their Sun sign. So you may have your Sun in Cancer, and all that means, but this might be countered by a strong-willed and stubborn Moon in Taurus; or you may have your Sun in open-hearted Leo, but a Moon in Aquarius with all its rebellious, emotional detachment.

Phases of the Moon

The Moon orbits the Earth, taking roughly 28 days to do so. How much of the Moon we see is determined by how much of the Sun's light it reflects, giving us the impression that it waxes, or grows, and wanes. When the Moon is new, to us, only a sliver of it is illuminated. As it waxes, it reflects more light and moves from a crescent, to a waxing crescent to a first quarter; then it moves to a waxing gibbous Moon, to a full Moon. Then the Moon begins to wane through a waning gibbous, to a last quarter, and then the cycle begins again. All of this occurs over four weeks. When we have two full Moons in any one calendar month, the second is called a blue Moon.

Each month the Moon also moves through an astrological sign, as we know from our personal birth charts. This, too, will yield information – a Moon in Scorpio can have a very different effect to one in Capricorn – and depending on our personal charts, this can have a shifting influence each month. For example, if the Moon in your birth chart is in Virgo, then when the actual Moon moves into Virgo, this will have an additional influence. Read the characteristics of the signs for further information (see pages 12–17).

The Moon's cycle has an energetic effect, which we can see quite easily on the ocean tides. Astrologically, because the Moon is both a fertility symbol and attuned to our deeper psychological side, we can use this to focus more profoundly and creatively on aspects of life that are important to us.

Eclipses

Generally speaking, an eclipse covers up and prevents light being shed on a situation. Astrologically speaking, this will depend on where the Sun or Moon is positioned in relation to other planets at the time of an eclipse. So if a solar eclipse is in Gemini, there will be a Geminian influence or an influence on Geminis.

Hiding, or shedding, light on an area of our lives is an invitation to pay attention to it. Eclipses are generally about beginnings or endings, which is why our ancestors saw them as portents, important signs to be taken notice of. As it is possible to know when an eclipse is forthcoming, these are charted astronomically; consequently, their astrological significance can be assessed and acted upon ahead of time.

The 10 planets

For the purpose of astrology (but not for astronomy, because the Sun is really a star) we talk about 10 planets, and each astrological sign has a ruling planet, with Mercury, Venus and Mars each being assigned two. The characteristics of each planet describe those influences that can affect signs, all of which information feeds into the interpretation of a birth chart.

The Moon

This sign is an opposing principle to the Sun, forming a pair, and it represents the feminine, symbolising containment and receptivity, how we react most instinctively and with feeling.

Rules the sign of Cancer.

The Sun

The Sun represents the masculine, and is seen as the energy that sparks life, which suggests a paternal energy in our birth chart. It also symbolises our self or essential being, and our purpose.

Rules the sign of Leo.

Mercury

Mercury is the planet of communication and symbolises our urge to make sense of, understand and communicate our thoughts through words.

Rules the signs of Gemini and Virgo.

Venus

The planet of love is all about
attraction, connection and pleasure
and in a female chart it symbolises
her style of femininity, while in a male
chart it represents his ideal partner.

Rules the signs of Taurus and Libra.

Mars

This planet symbolises pure energy
(Mars was, after all, the god of War)
but it also tells you in which areas
you're most likely to be assertive,
aggressive or to take risks.

Rules the signs of Aries and Scorpio.

Saturn

Saturn is sometimes called the wise teacher or taskmaster of astrology, symbolising lessons learnt and limitations, showing us the value of determination, tenacity and resilience.

Rules the sign of Capricorn.

Jupiter

The planet Jupiter is the largest in our solar system and symbolises bounty and benevolence, all that is expansive and jovial. Like the sign it rules, it's also about moving away from the home on journeys and exploration.

Rules the sign of Sagittarius.

Uranus

This planet symbolises the unexpected, new ideas and innovation, and the urge to tear down the old and usher in the new. The downside can mark an inability to fit in and consequently the feeling of being an outsider.

Rules the sign of Aquarius.

Pluto

Aligned to Hades (*Pluto* in Latin), the god of the underworld or death, the planet exerts a powerful force that lies below the surface and which, in its most negative form, can represent obsessions and compulsive behaviour.

Rules the sign of Scorpio.

Neptune

Linked to the sea, this is about what lies beneath, underwater and too deep to be seen clearly. Sensitive, intuitive and artistic, it also symbolises the capacity to love unconditionally, to forgive and forget.

Rules the sign of Pisces.

The four elements

Further divisions of the 12 astrological signs into the four elements of earth, fire, air and water yield other characteristics. This comes from ancient Greek medicine, where the body was considered to be made up of four bodily fluids or 'humours'. These four humours – blood, yellow bile, black bile and phlegm – corresponded to the four temperaments of sanguine, choleric, melancholic and phlegmatic, to the four seasons of the year, spring, summer, autumn, winter, and the four elements of air, fire, earth and water.

Related to astrology, these symbolic qualities cast further light on characteristics of the different signs. Carl Jung also used them in his psychology, and we still refer to people as earthy, fiery, airy or wet in their approach to life, while sometimes describing people as 'being in their element'. In astrology, those Sun signs that share the same element are said to have an affinity, or an understanding, with each other.

Like all aspects of astrology, there is always a positive and a negative, and a knowledge of any 'shadow side' can be helpful in terms of self-knowledge and what we may need to enhance or balance out, particularly in our dealings with others.

Air

GEMINI ✷ LIBRA ✷ AQUARIUS

Fire

ARIES ✷ LEO ✷ SAGITTARIUS

The realm of ideas is where these air signs excel. Perceptive and visionary and able to see the big picture, there is a very reflective quality to air signs that helps to vent situations. Too much air, however, can dissipate intentions, so Gemini might be indecisive, Libra has a tendency to sit on the fence, while Aquarius can be very disengaged.

There is a warmth and energy to these signs, a positive approach, spontaneity and enthusiasm that can be inspiring and very motivational to others. The downside is that Aries has a tendency to rush in headfirst, Leo can have a need for attention and Sagittarius can tend to talk it up but not deliver.

Earth

TAURUS ✱ VIRGO ✱ CAPRICORN

Characteristically, these signs enjoy sensual pleasure, enjoying food and other physical pleasures, and they like to feel grounded, preferring to base their ideas in facts. The downside is that Taureans can be stubborn, Virgos can be pernickety and Capricorns can veer towards a dogged conservatism.

Water

CANCER ✱ SCORPIO ✱ PISCES

Water signs are very responsive, like the tide ebbing and flowing, and can be very perceptive and intuitive, sometimes uncannily so because of their ability to feel. The downside is – watery enough – a tendency to feel swamped, and then Cancer can be both tenacious and self-protective, Pisces chameleon-like in their attention and Scorpio unpredictable and intense.

Cardinal, fixed and mutable signs

In addition to the 12 signs being divided into four elements, they can also be grouped into three different ways in which their energies may act or react, giving further depth to each sign's particular characteristics.

Cardinal

ARIES ✳ CANCER ✳ LIBRA ✳ CAPRICORN

These are action planets, with an energy that takes the initiative and gets things started. Aries has the vision, Cancer the feelings, Libra the contacts and Capricorn the strategy.

Fixed

TAURUS ✳ LEO ✳ SCORPIO ✳ AQUARIUS

Slower but more determined, these signs work to progress and maintain those initiatives that the cardinal signs have fired up. Taurus offers physical comfort, Leo loyalty, Scorpio emotional support and Aquarius sound advice. You can count on fixed signs, but they tend to resist change.

Mutable

GEMINI ✳ VIRGO ✳ SAGITTARIUS ✳ PISCES

Adaptable and responsive to new ideas, places and people, mutable signs have a unique ability to adjust to their surroundings. Gemini is mentally agile, Virgo is practical and versatile, Sagittarius visualises possibilities and Pisces is responsive to change.

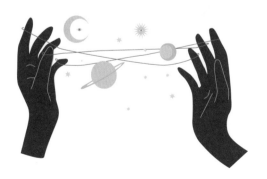

The 12 houses

The birth chart is divided into 12 houses, which represent separate areas and functions of your life. When you are told you have something in a specific house – for example, Libra (balance) in the fifth house (creativity and sex) – it creates a way of interpreting the influences that can arise and are particular to how you might approach an aspect of your life.

Each house relates to a Sun sign, and in this way each is represented by some of the characteristics of that sign, which is said to be its natural ruler.

Three of these houses are considered to be mystical, relating to our interior, psychic world: the fourth (home), eighth (death and regeneration) and twelfth (secrets).

1ˢᵗ House

THE SELF

RULED BY ARIES

This house symbolises the self: you, who you are and how you represent yourself, your likes, dislikes and approach to life. It also represents how you see yourself and what you want in life.

2ⁿᵈ House

POSSESSIONS

RULED BY TAURUS

The second house symbolises your possessions, what you own, including money; how you earn or acquire your income; and your material security and the physical things you take with you as you move through life.

3ʳᵈ House

COMMUNICATION

RULED BY GEMINI

This house is about communication and mental attitude, primarily how you express yourself. It's also about how you function within your family, and how you travel to school or work, and includes how you think, speak, write and learn.

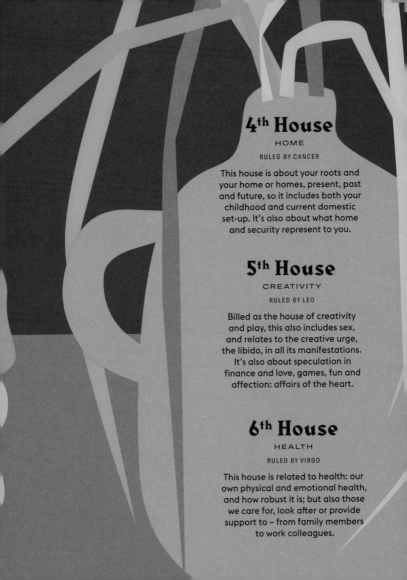

4th House

HOME

RULED BY CANCER

This house is about your roots and your home or homes, present, past and future, so it includes both your childhood and current domestic set-up. It's also about what home and security represent to you.

5th House

CREATIVITY

RULED BY LEO

Billed as the house of creativity and play, this also includes sex, and relates to the creative urge, the libido, in all its manifestations. It's also about speculation in finance and love, games, fun and affection: affairs of the heart.

6th House

HEALTH

RULED BY VIRGO

This house is related to health: our own physical and emotional health, and how robust it is; but also those we care for, look after or provide support to – from family members to work colleagues.

7th House

PARTNERSHIPS

RULED BY LIBRA

The opposite of the first house, this reflects shared goals and
intimate partnerships, our choice of life partner and how
successful our relationships might be. It also reflects
partnerships and adversaries in our professional world.

8th House

REGENERATION

RULED BY SCORPIO

For death, read regeneration or spiritual transformation: this
house also reflects legacies and what you inherit after death,
in personality traits or materially. And because regeneration
requires sex, it's also about sex and sexual emotions.

9th House

TRAVEL

RULED BY SAGITTARIUS

The house of long-distance travel and exploration, this is also
about the broadening of the mind that travel can bring, and
how that might express itself. It also reflects the sending out of
ideas, which can come about from literary effort or publication.

11th House

FRIENDSHIPS

RULED BY AQUARIUS

The eleventh house is about friendship groups and acquaintances, vision and ideas, and is less about immediate gratification but more concerning longer-term dreams and how these might be realised through our ability to work harmoniously with others.

12th House

SECRETS

RULED BY PISCES

Considered the most spiritual house, it is also the house of the unconscious, of secrets and of what might lie hidden, the metaphorical skeleton in the closet. It also reflects the secret ways we might self-sabotage or imprison our own efforts by not exploring them.

10th House

ASPIRATIONS

RULED BY CAPRICORN

This represents our aspiration and status, how we'd like to be elevated in public standing (or not), our ambitions, image and what we'd like to attain in life, through our own efforts.

The ascendant

Otherwise known as your rising sign, this is the sign of the zodiac that appears at the horizon as dawn breaks on the day of your birth, depending on your location in the world and time of birth. This is why knowing your time of birth is a useful factor in astrology, because your 'rising sign' yields a lot of information about those aspects of your character that are more on show, how you present yourself and how you are seen by others. So, even if you are a Sun Cancer, but have Sagittarius rising, you may be seen as someone who is freewheeling, with a noticeable taste for adventure in one way or another. Knowing your own ascendant – or that of another person – will often help explain why there doesn't seem to be such a direct correlation between their personality and their Sun sign.

As long as you know your time of birth and where you were born, working out your ascendant using an online tool or app is very easy (see page 108). Just ask your mum or other family members, or check your birth certificate (in those countries that include a birth time). If the astrological chart were a clock face, the ascendant would be at the 9 o'clock position.

The descendant

The descendant gives an indication of a possible life partner, based on the idea that opposites attract. Once you know your ascendant, the descendant is easy to work out as it is always six signs away: for example, if your ascendant is Virgo, your descendant is Pisces. If the astrological chart were a clock face, the descendant would be at the 3 o'clock position.

The midheaven (MC)

Also included in the birth chart is the position of the midheaven or MC (from the Latin, *medium coeli*, meaning middle of the heavens), which indicates your attitude towards your work, career and professional standing. If the astrological chart were a clock face, the MC would be at the 12 o'clock position.

The IC

Finally, your IC (from the Latin, *imum coeli*, meaning the lowest part of the heavens) indicates your attitude towards your home and family, and is also related to the end of your life. Your IC will be directly opposite your MC: for example, if your MC is Aquarius, your IC is Leo. If the astrological chart were a clock face, the IC would be at the 6 o'clock position.

Saturn return

Saturn is one of the slower-moving planets, taking around 28 years to complete its orbit around the Sun and return to the place it occupied at the time of your birth. This return can last between two to three years and be very noticeable in the period coming up to our thirtieth and sixtieth birthdays, often considered to be significant 'milestone' birthdays.

Because the energy of Saturn is sometimes experienced as demanding, this isn't always an easy period of life. A wise teacher or a hard taskmaster, some consider the Saturn effect as 'cruel to be kind' in the way that many good teachers can be, keeping us on track like a rigorous personal trainer.

Everyone experiences their Saturn return relevant to their circumstances, but it is a good time to take stock, let go of the stuff in your life that no longer serves you and revise your expectations, while being unapologetic about what you would like to include more of in your life. So if you are experiencing or anticipating this life event, embrace and work with it because what you learn now – about yourself, mainly – is worth knowing, however turbulent it might be, and can pay dividends in how you manage the next 28 years!

Mercury retrograde

Even those with little interest in astrology often take notice when the planet Mercury is retrograde. Astrologically, retrogrades are periods when planets are stationary but, as we continue to move forwards, Mercury 'appears' to move backwards. There is a shadow period either side of a retrograde period, when it could be said to be slowing down or speeding up, which can also be a little turbulent. Generally speaking, the advice is not to make any important moves related to communication on a retrograde and, even if a decision is made, know that it's likely to change.

Given that Mercury is the planet of communication, you can immediately see why there are concerns about its retrograde status and its link to communication failures – of the old-fashioned sort when the post office loses a letter, or the more modern technological variety when your computer crashes

– causing problems. Mercury retrograde can also affect travel, with delays in flights or train times, traffic jams or collisions. Mercury also influences personal communications: listening, speaking, being heard (or not), and can cause confusion or arguments. It can also affect more formal agreements, like contracts between buyer and seller.

These retrograde periods occur three to four times a year, lasting for roughly three weeks, with a shadow period either side. The dates in which it happens also mean it occurs within a specific astrological sign. If, for example, it occurs between 25 October and 15 November, its effect would be linked to the characteristics of Scorpio. In addition, those Sun sign Scorpios, or those with Scorpio in significant placements in their chart, may also experience a greater effect.

Mercury retrograde dates are easy to find from an astrological table, or ephemeris, and online. These can be used in order to avoid planning events that might be affected around these times. How Mercury retrograde may affect you more personally requires knowledge of your birth chart and an understanding of its more specific combination of influences with the signs and planets in your chart.

If you are going to weather a Mercury retrograde more easily, be aware that glitches can occur so, to some extent, expect delays and double-check details. Stay positive if postponements occur and consider this period an opportunity to slow down, review or reconsider ideas in your business or your personal life. Use the time to correct mistakes or reshape plans, preparing for when any stuck energy can shift and you can move forward again more smoothly.

Further reading

Astrology Decoded (2013)
by Sue Merlyn Farebrother;
published by Rider

Astrology for Dummies
(2007) by Rae Orion;
published by Wiley Publishing

*Chart Interpretation
Handbook: Guidelines for
Understanding the Essentials
of the Birth Chart* (1990)
by Stephen Arroyo;
published by CRCS
Publications

Jung's Studies in Astrology
(2018) by Liz Greene;
published by RKP

*The Only Astrology
Book You'll Ever Need*
(2012) by Joanne Woolfolk;
published by Taylor Trade

Websites

astro.com

astrologyzone.com

jessicaadams.com

shelleyvonstrunkel.com

Apps

Astrostyle

Co-Star

Susan Miller's Astrology Zone

The Daily Horoscope

The Pattern

Time Passages

Acknowledgements

Particular thanks are due to my trusty team of Taureans. Firstly, to Kate Pollard, Publishing Director at Hardie Grant, for her passion for beautiful books and for commissioning this series. And to Bex Fitzsimons for all her good natured and conscientious editing. And finally to Evi O. Studio, whose illustration and design talents have produced small works of art. With such a star-studded team, these books can only shine and for that, my thanks.

About the author

Stella Andromeda has been studying
astrology for over 30 years, believing that
a knowledge of the constellations of the
skies and their potential for psychological
interpretation can be a useful tool. This
extension of her study into book form makes
modern insights about the ancient wisdom
of the stars easily accessible, sharing her
passion that reflection and self-knowledge
only empowers us in life. With her sun in
Taurus, Aquarius ascendant and Moon
in Cancer, she utilises earth, air and water
to inspire her own astrological journey.

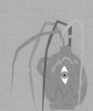

Published in 2019 by Hardie Grant Books,
an imprint of Hardie Grant Publishing

Hardie Grant Books (London)
5th & 6th Floors
52–54 Southwark Street
London SE1 1UN

Hardie Grant Books (Melbourne)
Building 1, 658 Church Street
Richmond, Victoria 3121

hardiegrantbooks.com

British Library Cataloguing-in-Publication Data. A catalogue record
for this book is available from the British Library.

Cancer
ISBN: 9781784882716

10 9 8 7 6 5

Publishing Director: Kate Pollard
Junior Editor: Bex Fitzsimons
Art Direction and Illustrations: Evi O. Studio
Editor: Wendy Hobson
Production Controller: Sinead Hering

Colour reproduction by p2d
Printed and bound in China by Leo Paper Products Ltd.